Tell Me About You: Dad

By

D. Rackley

Copyright © D. Rackley 2021
All Rights Reserved

Introduction

Dear Dad,

This book is for all those questions I might not have the answers to and the questions I might not have asked. I want a piece of your mind to keep with me forever. There are a few rules I would like you to follow so we can both get the most out of this book. They are as follows:

1) Be deliberate.

Please don't feel like you need to rush and answer (unless time permits). Think of what your answer might be like and ponder it. This is an exercise for you as well as to allow me to get know you on a deeper level.

2) Give as much detail as possible.

I'd appreciate as much detail as possible; I would love to know the ins and outs of your thoughts/memories. Please don't be short on your answers, as some of these questions may never come up between us again.

3) Don't hold back.

Don't feel like you can't reveal some information for one reason or another. All questions are to be answered as honestly as possible as not to insult your own memory and thoughts. Try to answer all the questions (and give a response even in the irrelevant ones) as best you can.

4) Give the book back within one year.

A time limit is to make sure you are giving answers consistent to your state of mind in this very moment. Over many years, your memory may fade more or your viewpoints on life and its circumstances may change considerably.

5) Have fun.

The most important rule is to have fun. Enjoy this book as you relive your life and ponder the world. I can't wait to get it back as an awesome gift to me. The more you enjoy the process, the more I will be able to see it in your writing. Feel free to customise this book to your liking, draw in the corners and make it your own if you wish. This book is a piece of you.

Ready? Here it begins. Let's start at the beginning...

Childhood (0-12 years)

Introduction to life

What's the story of your birth?

What's the story of your name?

What is your earliest childhood memory?

Where did you grow up?

Describe your living circumstances as a child?

Relationships with others

Tell me about your parents

What was your relationship with your parents like growing up?

What are some of the most important lessons you learned from your parents?

Tell me about your grandparents

What was your relationship with your grandparents like growing up?

What are some important lessons you learned from your grandparents?

What was something you learned from interacting with people outside your immediate family?

Tell me about your siblings

What was your relationship like with your siblings?

What family member were you closest to? Why?

Who were your childhood best friends/companions?

Who had the biggest impact on your personality?

Did you have any pets growing up?

Child's Mind

What were some childhood dreams you had?

What were some of the hardest moments you experienced as a child?

What did you want to do for a living as a child? Why?

What were you most scared of?

What didn't make sense to you as much as you tried to understand it?

Interactions with the world

What were your favourite things to do as a child?

Where was your favourite place to go as a child?

Did you ever break any rules? If so, what did you do?

What was your favourite childhood movie? Why?

Did you play any sports growing up? If so, tell me more

What talents were you most gifted among your peers with?

What was your favourite music to listen to as a child? What was played in your household?

Reflection

What was a major turning point in your childhood? Why?

Is there anything that you missed out on as a child?

If you could have said anything to your adult self, what would you have said?

If you could speak to your child self now, what would you say?

When did you know you had crossed into adolescence?

Adolescence & Young Adulthood

Adolescence & Young Adulthood (12-21)

Shaping your personality

Who had the most influence on you?

_____
_____
_____
_____
_____
_____
_____
_____
_____
_____
_____
_____
_____
_____
_____

What experience had the most influence on you?

What piece of media (ie. book, radio broadcast, tv show, music) had the most influence on you? Why?

Who did you go to for advice growing up? In hindsight, were they correct or wrong?

The Adolescent Experience

What was some of your favourite music?

Tell me a funny story that you still laugh about today

_____
_____
_____
_____
_____
_____
_____
_____
_____
_____
_____
_____
_____
_____
_____
_____
_____
_____
_____
_____
_____
_____
_____

What are you proud to have accomplished growing up?

What were your usual weekends like?

Is there anything that you feel hasn't changed between our adolescence?

What's an embarrassing thing/moment your mum or dad did?

What's your opinion on your hometown?

What was your relationship like with your siblings at this point of time?

Your early life firsts

What's the first album you ever bought? Do you still listen to them?

Who was your first kiss? What was the story?

Where was your first vacation to? Tell me about it

What was your first major purchase? Why'd you spend it on that?

Where was your first job? Tell me about it

Molding your life

What did you envision for your adulthood at this stage?

_____

_____

_____

_____

_____

_____

_____

_____

_____

_____

_____

_____

_____

_____

_____

_____

_____

_____

_____

Did you cut any friends from your circle? If so, why?

What's the dumbest thing you did as an adolescent? What did you learn?

What is something that felt right at the time, but turned out to be a mistake?

Do you have any regrets during this time? If so, how would things have been different if you did/didn't do them?

When did you know you crossed into adulthood?

Adulthood

Adulthood (21+)

Relationships, Things & Experiences

How did you meet my mother?

_____
_____
_____
_____
_____
_____
_____
_____
_____
_____
_____
_____
_____
_____
_____
_____
_____

In your opinion, what is essential to a successful relationship/marriage?

What was the hardest /breaking point in your relationship with my mother?

What was the best moment between you and my mother?

Tell me about the relationship with your parents during adulthood

Tell me about the relationship with your siblings/other close family members during adulthood

What was something you threw away that you wish you had today?

What is your favourite movie? Why?

Who is your favourite musician/band? Why?

What is the most memorable lesson you learned from your parents? How has it helped you?

What has been the best book you have ever read?

What's the best gift you've ever received?

What's the best gift you've ever given?

Best place you have ever travelled to? Why?

Places you would like to visit but have not yet?

Adult Life

What has been the best thing about being an adult?

What is the hardest thing about being an adult?

What are you most proud of to have accomplished?

What are some of the most amazing things you have experienced?

What is something you look forward to every day?

What was the best live event that you went to?

What is your most embarrassing moment?

What are the biggest turning points of your adulthood? Why?

What are some habits that you wish you could kick? Why can't you?

What are some habits that you're thankful you have?

What would you consider to be your best personality trait?

Have you used any illegal drugs?

What is your dream job?

What was the greatest day of your life so far?

The Adult Mind

What is your definition of the 'meaning of life'?

Did you end up where you thought you'd be?

What do you know is an absolute fact?

If you could have dinner with 3 people (dead or alive) who would it be and why?

What did you take for granted?

What is your greatest obstacle in life? How have you overcome it or learned to deal with it?

What memory instantly makes you smile?

What is a quote that you live by?

What would be the soundtrack of your life? Why?

Philosophical Thoughts

What do you believe happens when we die?

_____
_____
_____
_____
_____
_____
_____
_____
_____
_____
_____
_____
_____
_____

If you had 100 million dollars, how would you spend it?

Have you ever experienced anything paranormal?

Do you believe the world is good/bad or just has both elements in it?

What do you believe we were before our birth?

What do you think is essential to have to live a happy life? Why?

Are you a product of your environment or born the way you are? Why?

Do you believe there is life on another planet?

What is the most important trait someone can have? Why?

What would make the world a better place? Why?

Can you have happiness without sadness?

What is love?

If you are born again, what animal would you like to be? Why?

If you are born again, what country would you like it to be? Why?

Is suffering part of the human condition? Does hardship make people stronger?

How do you deal with stress?

What's a social or political cause you're most passionate about? Why?

What are your political views? How do you think they were formed?

How would you describe your relationship with money?

If you could rid the world of one thing, what would it be? Why?

What is your definition of a man?

About Us

About Us

Tell me the story of my name

___

How did you find out mum was pregnant with me? What was your reaction?

Tell me the story of the day I was born

What was the most difficult thing about raising me/siblings?

What would be the best parenting advice you can give?

What lessons did you learn as a parent?

Tell me something random about you that I would not know

What's something you wish you could have told me as a kid, but couldn't? Why?

Is there anything in our family that you've kept a secret?

What has been the best gift I have ever given you?

What did I do as a child that frustrated you?

What did I do as a child that made you laugh?

What do I do now that makes you laugh?

When was the first time you heard me swear?

What song reminds you of me most?

What do I do that makes you upset? Why?

What is your proudest moment of me?

What did you think I would be when I grew up?

In what ways are we similar?

In what ways are we different?

What is a piece of advice you have for my life?

Where should I look for you when you're not around?

What is your hope for me?

What is your favourite moment of us together?

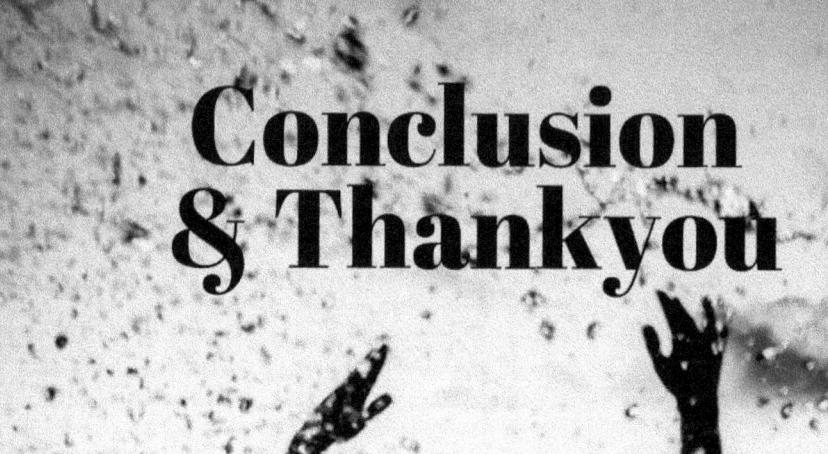

Conclusion

There is just one thing left to do in this book. I would like you to leave me a surprise in this book or give a priceless gift when you return the book back to me. Just for some ideas, it could be a photo of us that you love, a small sentimental item, a family recipe etc.

Thank you for spending your time answering my questions, I believe this will be a book that I cherish forever. I love you.

www.ingramcontent.com/pod-product-compliance
Ingram Content Group UK Ltd.
Pitfield, Milton Keynes, MK11 3LW, UK
UKHW022240230426
12048UKWH00018BA/1365